Team Strings

An integrated course for individual, group and mixed instrument teaching

Violin

Richard Duckett, Olive Goodborn & Christopher Rogers

Melissa Griffin

New violin Exam Book Grade 3
100 solos for the violin

James Ross (0121) 643 7623

Published by
International Music Publications Ltd
Griffin House 161 Hammersmith Road London England W6 8BS

Edited by BARRIE CARSON TURNER

Piano accompaniments by BARRIE CARSON TURNER

Sincere thanks are extended to the following people:
CHRISTOPHER BULL, author and arranger of ensemble TEAM STRINGS BOOK 1, for the original plan for TEAM STRINGS BOOK 2.
CELIA DOUBLEDAY, cellist, who worked on the material in preparation.
ANN GOODBORN, double bass tutor who worked with Christopher Bull on ideas for the original draft.
MONICA HERMOLLE, cellist, for her invaluable support in the preparation of these books.
BRIAN LESTER, Birmingham Instrumental Team, for his invaluable advise and support.
SHELAGH REID, violinist and teacher (Aberdeen), for her invaluable advise on technical matters and repertoire.
JENNY SMITH, violinist and teacher (Worcestershire), for her invaluable advise and support.
LORNA WINDASS, violinist and teacher (Addenburgh, Oxfordshire), for her invaluable support and help on bowing the material.

First published 2002

Music engraving and typesetting: Barnes Music Engraving Ltd, East Sussex TN34 1HA

Contents

Team Strings 2 Ensemble

TEAM STRINGS 2 ensemble material has been specially written so that it can be played by almost any combination of string instruments the teacher may encounter.

On each ensemble page there are three or four parts. The first is the melody and the second is a duet part. The third and fourth parts are either a bass line, a harmony part or a descant. Each piece can therefore be used as a solo, duet, trio, or quartet with or without piano accompaniment.

By allocating the parts to different instruments it is easy to create a considerable variety of mixed ensembles, from a simple duet to a full string orchestra.

Each piece which can be played in emsemble or with a piano accompaniment also has the option of a CD backing track.

In addition to this, each piece can be extended into a longer one by varying the textures in subsequent verses. This can be done by reallocating the parts, playing in unison, using pizzicato accompaniments, introducing solo passages, etc.

The following symbols have been used to provide an immediate visual identification:

Pieces with piano accompaniment

Ensemble page
(score included in ACCOMPANIMENTS book)

☐ Pieces which appear in the same place on the same page in all four TEAM STRINGS 2 books

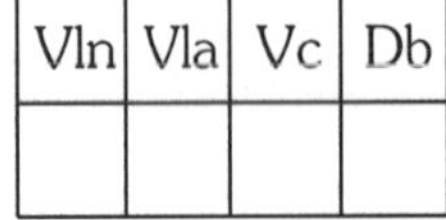

Vln	Vla	Vc	Db

The box to the left of each arrangement or score indicates where each piece can be found in the solo instrumental books.

Introducing Team Strings 2

As in TEAM STRINGS, TEAM STRINGS 2 has been designed to meet the needs of young string players everywhere, whether lessons are given individually, in groups or in the classroom.

Musical variety

TEAM STRINGS 2 has been specially designed to follow the original TEAM STRINGS TUTOR, although it can be used to follow on from any beginner string book. It offers the same wide variety of musical styles as the original, but is further enhanced by titles from the world of jazz and blues supported by a three-part course of improvisation techniques.

Ensemble pieces

TEAM STRINGS 2 offers corresponding pages of music which can be played in harmony for mixed string ensembles, from duet right up to full string orchestra. From page 43 onwards, TEAM STRINGS 2, TEAM BRASS, PERCUSSION and WOODWIND naturally share much of the same ensemble material allowing it to develop into full orchestra. As the TEAM STRINGS 2 tutors contain 25 pages of ensemble, they are suitable for school orchestra, string orchestra, symphony orchestra as well as solo, duet and other small groups.

Flexible course

TEAM STRINGS 2 does not offer guidance on how to play or teach a string instrument but rather offers material which the professional teacher can use to structure courses for individual pupils.

National Curriculum & GCSE skills

TEAM STRINGS 2 has been designed to help meet the requirements of the National Curriculum for music. In addition to fostering musical literacy, 'Play By Ear' lines provide early opportunities for composition and improvisation. This aspect of TEAM STRINGS can be a useful starting point for these elements in the GCSE examination course now followed by secondary schools.

Comprehensive notes on the use of this series, scores of the ensemble material, piano accompaniments and approaches to creative music making are given in the accompaniments book.

Accompaniments

Accompaniments for selected solo pieces, and the ensemble pieces, are available in the Accompaniments book and on the CD.

Lesson diary and practice chart

Date (week commencing)	Enter number of minutes practised							Teacher indicates which pages to study
	Mon	Tue	Wed	Thu	Fri	Sat	Sun	

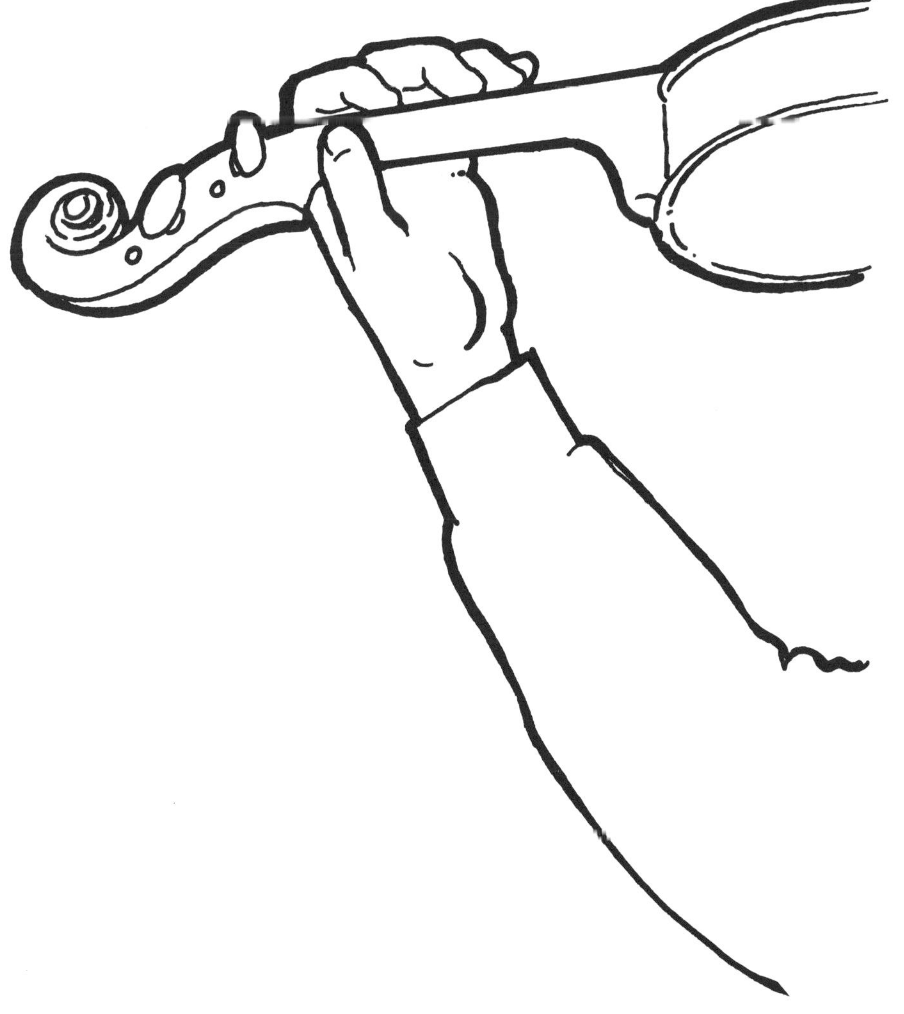

My grandfather's clock

4 clicks intro

Words and Music by
HENRY CLAY WORK (1832–1884)

Moderately

1\.

mp

mf

*

ff

The four dots mean
you can repeat the music
as often as you want

Moderately

2\.

mp

mf

*

ff

* Chime effect. Repeat chord 12 times, ad lib., and hold.

Heigh-ho

7 clicks intro

Words by LARRY MORLEY
Music by FRANK E. CHURCHILL

Simple gifts

Shaker melody

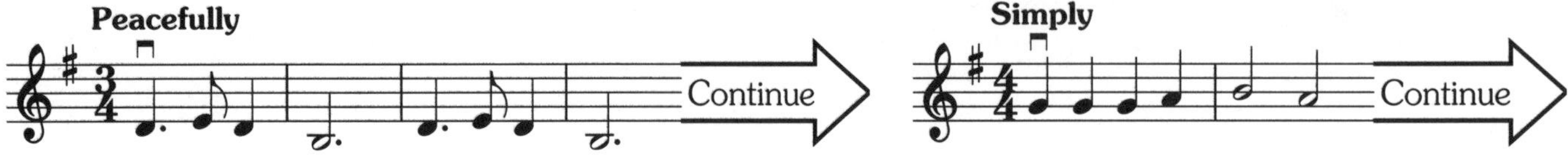

Daisy Bell

6 clicks intro

Words and Music by
HARRY DACRE (1860–1922)

Valse allegretto

G C G *mf*

9 D7 B7/D# Em A7 Am7 D7

17 Am7 D7 G G C G D7

25 G D7 G D7 G D7 G

rall.

rall. (rallentando) means gradually slowing down

If you're happy and you know it

Traditional

Sprightly

Oranges and lemons

Briskly

Traditional

The Lincolnshire poacher

Traditional

Slur study

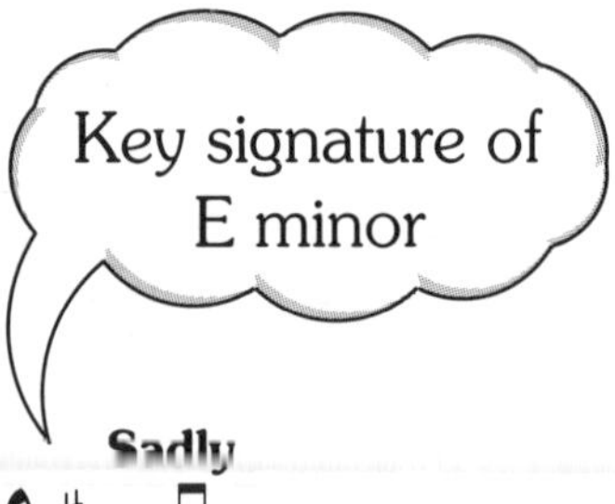

Melancholia

CHRISTOPHER BULL (1950–1994)

Sadly

mp

My Bonnie lies over the ocean

5 clicks intro

Traditional

With motion

1.

mf

1.

7

2.

p

15

1.

2.

With motion

2.

mf

1.

7

2.

p

15

1.

2.

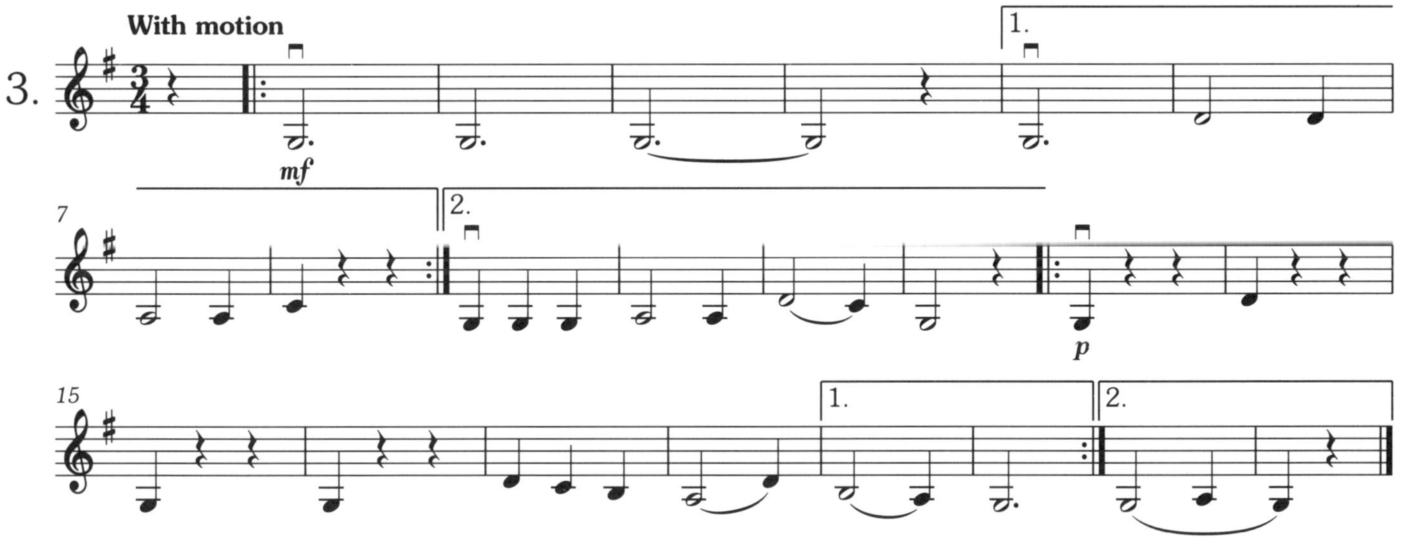

With motion

3.

mf

1.

7

2.

p

15

1.

2.

Staccato

Legato
means play the notes smoothly

Staccato
means play the notes short

Etude 1

Etude 2

Staccato duet

CHRISTOPHER BULL (1950–1994)

West Heath lilt

The cuckoo

EDWARD DUCKETT

Hornpipe

HENRY PURCELL (1659–1695)

Soldier, soldier

4 clicks intro

Traditional

March time
3.
f
to Coda
D.S. al Coda
CODA
March time
4.
f
to Coda
D.S. al Coda
CODA
Play by ear
Sprightly
Continue
Marziale
Continue

Broken slurs

Das Blumchen wunderhold

LUDWIG VAN BEETHOVEN (1770–1827)

Sleigh ride

CHRISTOPHER BULL (1950–1994)

Study 1

German tune

Traditional

Study 2

Minuet in G

HENRY PURCELL (1659–1695)

Rhythmic decoration

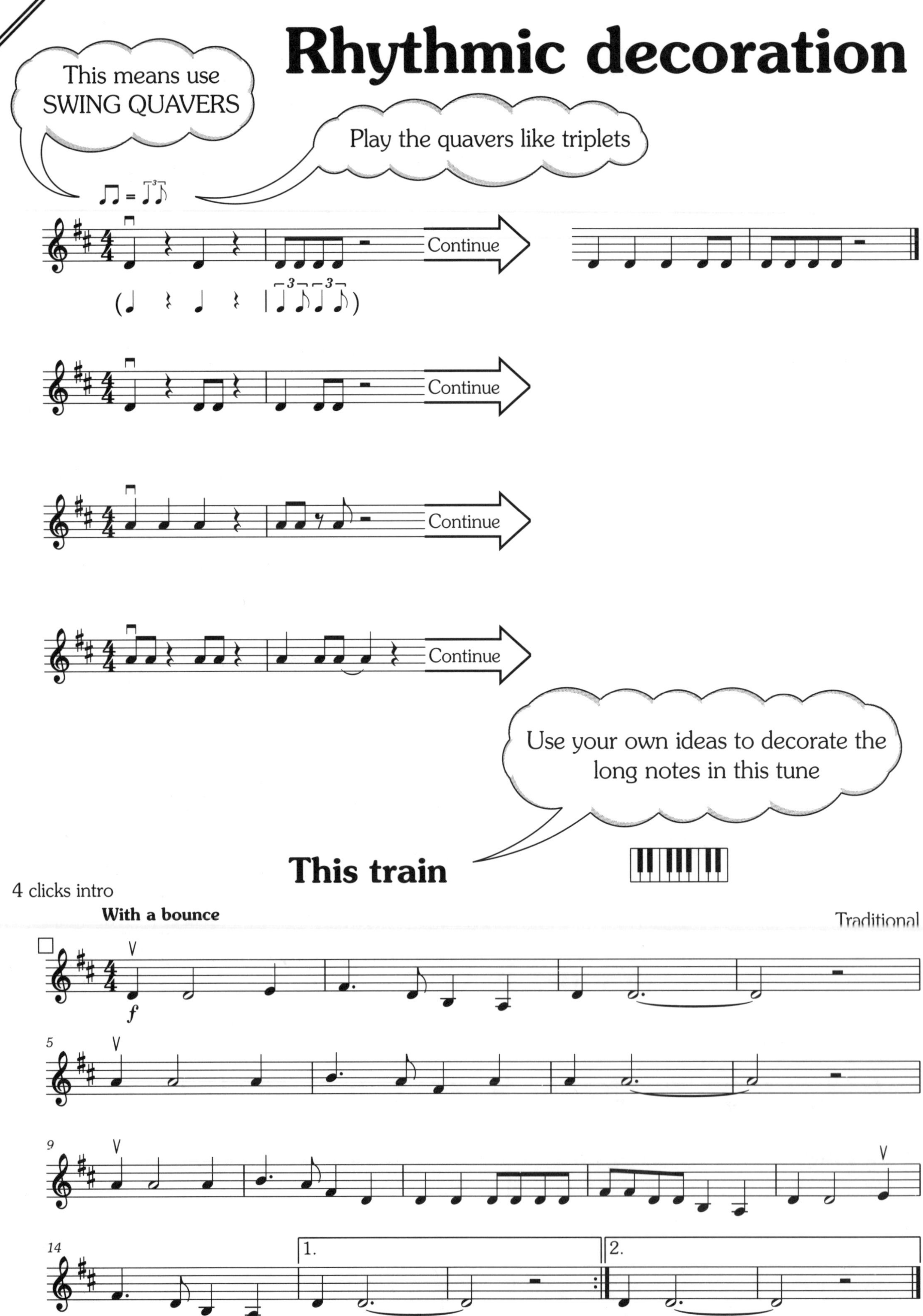

Take it away man

4 clicks intro

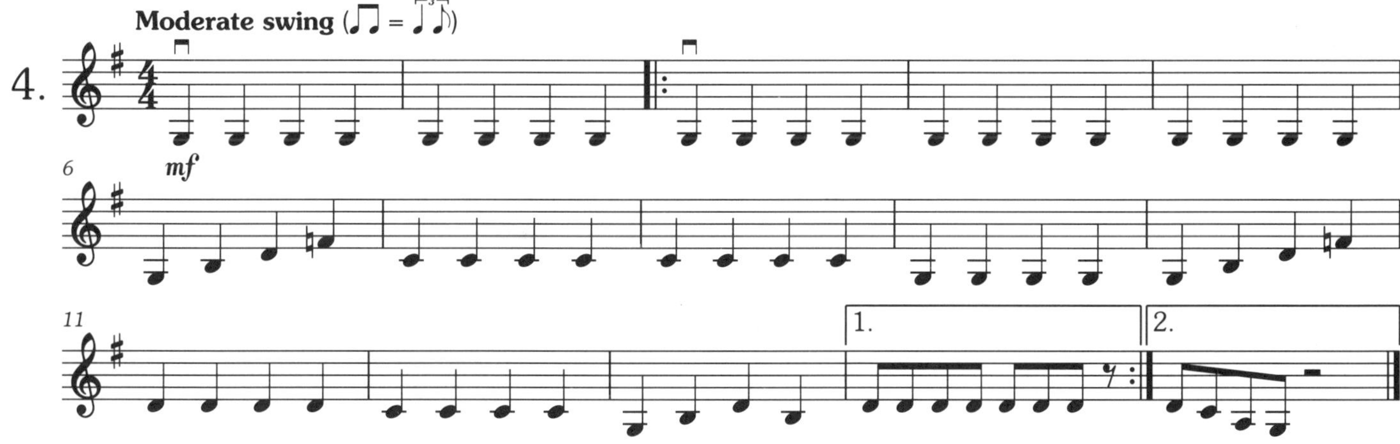

Cockles and mussels

Traditional

Hoch Wass' kommt von draussen Rhein

Traditional

Sailors' song

4 clicks intro

Traditional

The key of D major

Music in D major has a key signature of TWO sharps

L. A. nitespot

Twelve bar blues

Lasst uns erfreuen

Chorale melody

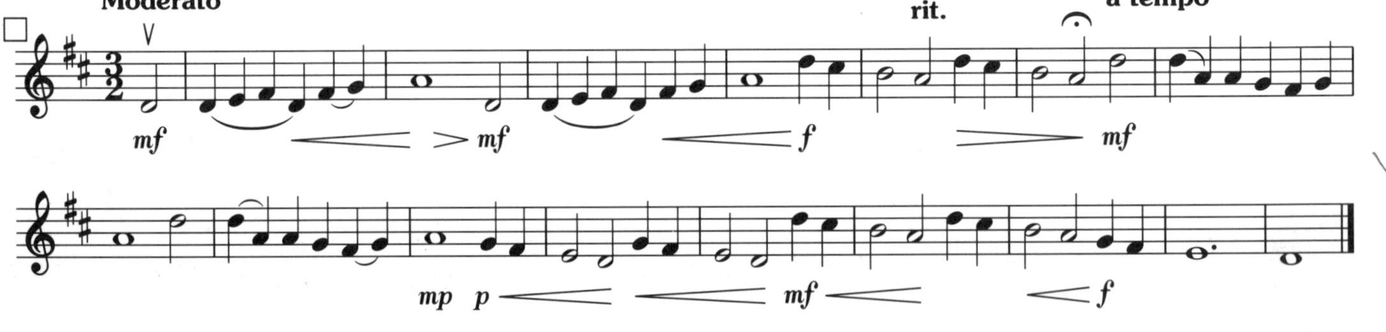

New world symphony

4 clicks intro

ANTONIN DVOŘÁK (1841–1904)

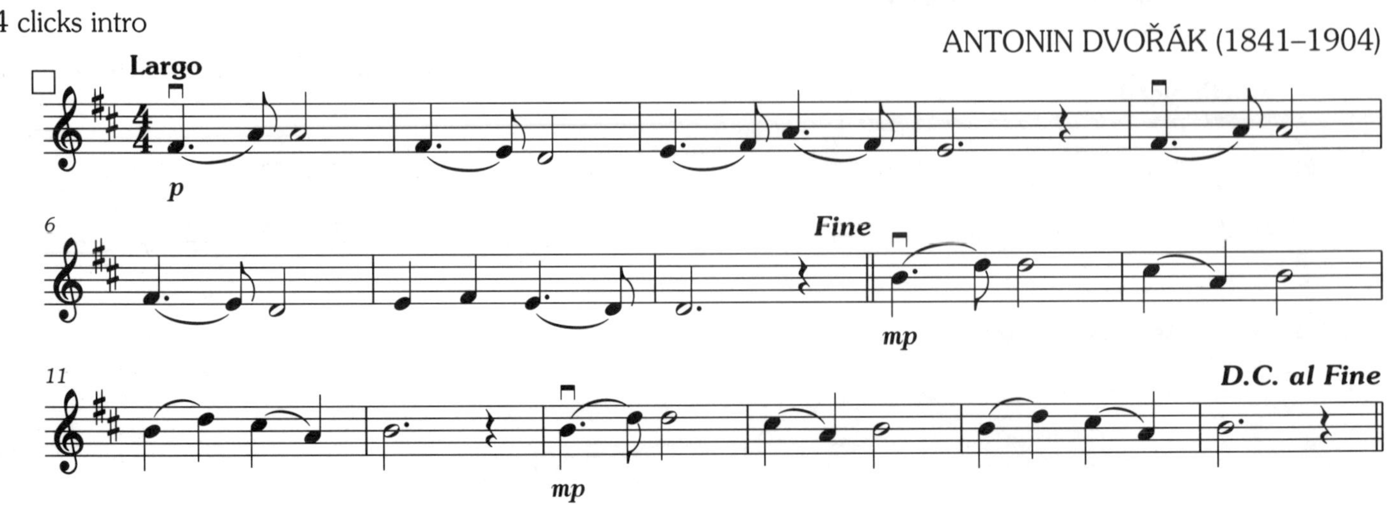

The rowan tree

3 clicks intro

Traditional

Swing low, sweet chariot

4 clicks intro

Traditional

Lullaby

5 clicks intro

JOHANNES BRAHMS (1833–1897)

For (s)he's a jolly good fellow

Comin' thro' the rye

Loch Lomond

3 clicks intro

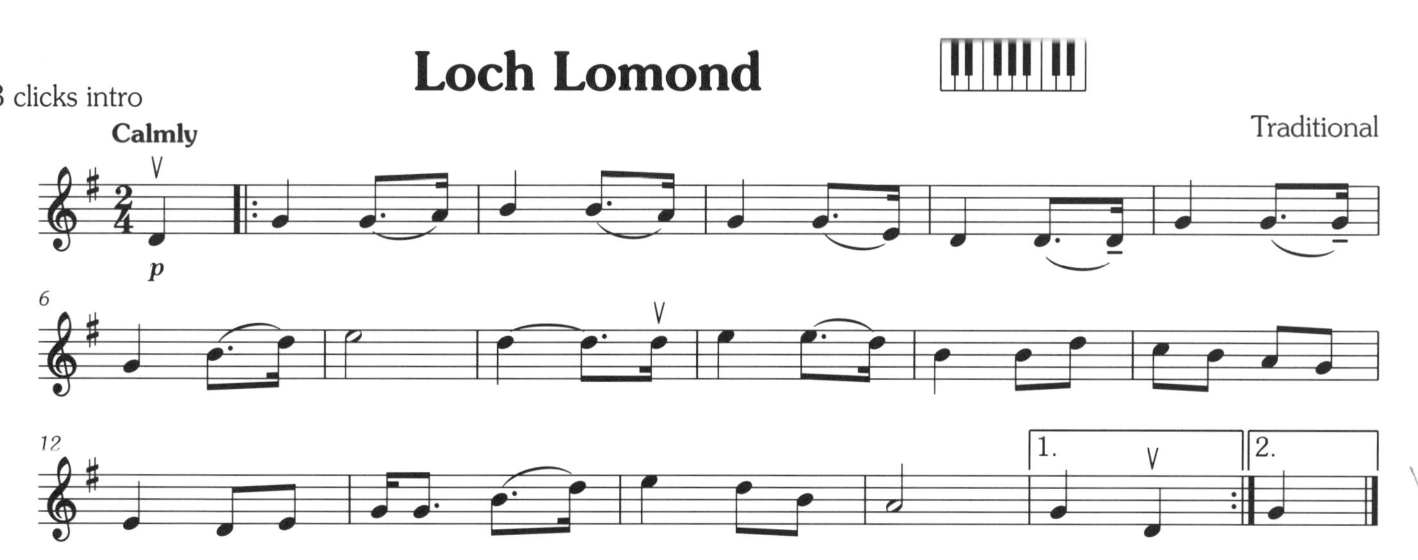

Scotland the brave

4 clicks intro

Play by ear

Moderato

Continue

I saw three ships

4 ♩. clicks intro

Traditional

Flowing

(Solo) (Tutti) (Solo)

1. *mf*

6 (Tutti) *Fine* *mf*

11 **D.C. al Fine**

Flowing

2. *mf*

6 *Fine* *mf*

11 **D.C. al Fine**

Flowing

3. *mf*

6 *Fine* *mf*

11 **D.C. al Fine**

Flowing

4. *mf*

6 *Fine*

11 *mf* **D.C. al Fine**

Joy to the world

4 clicks intro

GEORGE FREDERIC HANDEL (1685–1759)

Melodic improvisation

When the saints go marching in

5 clicks intro

Traditional

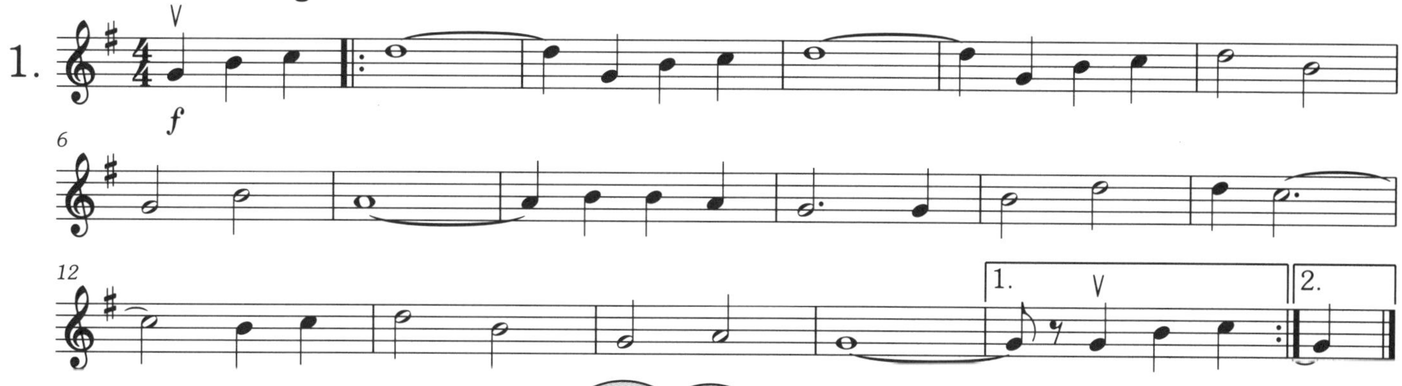

1. Medium swing

f

2. Medium swing

f

3. Medium swing

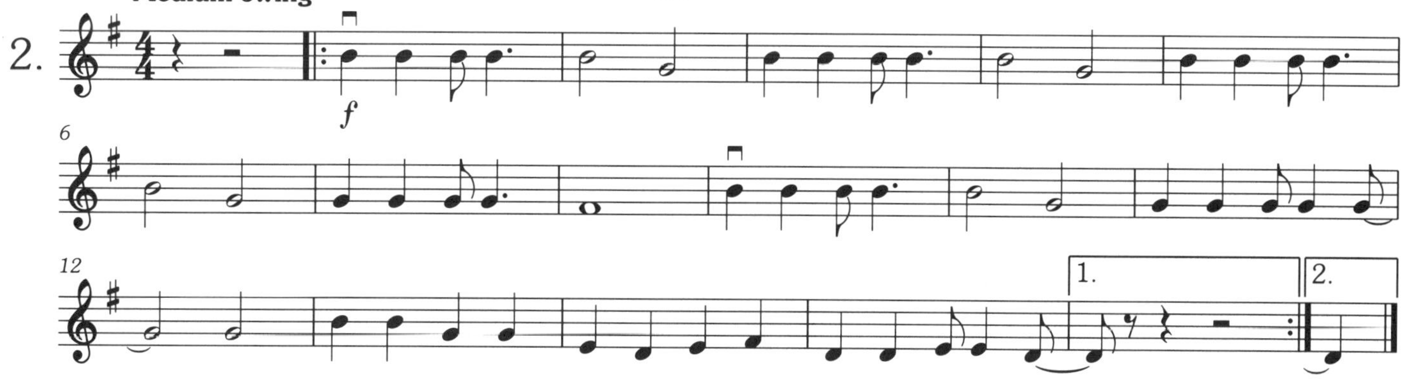

f

4. Medium swing

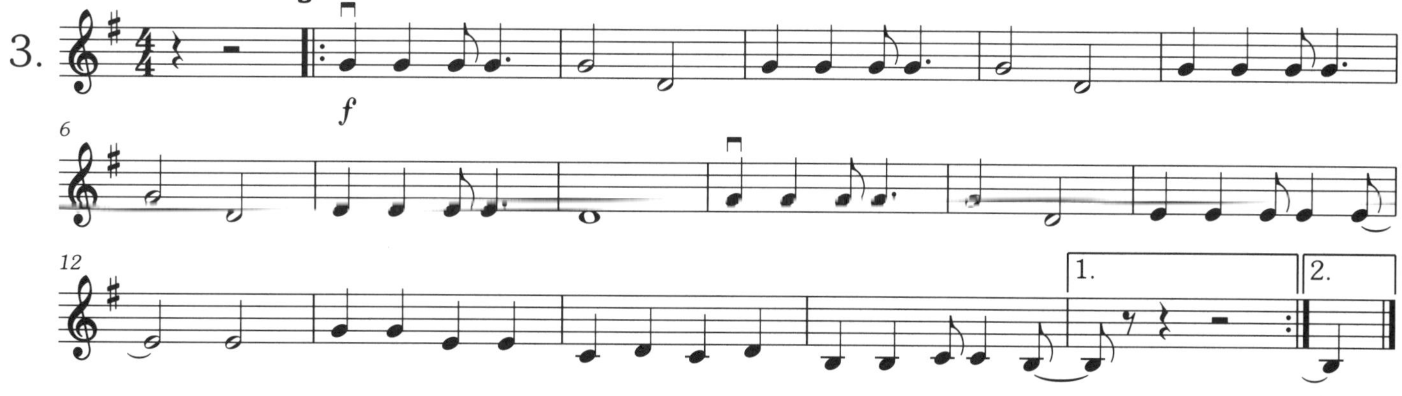

f

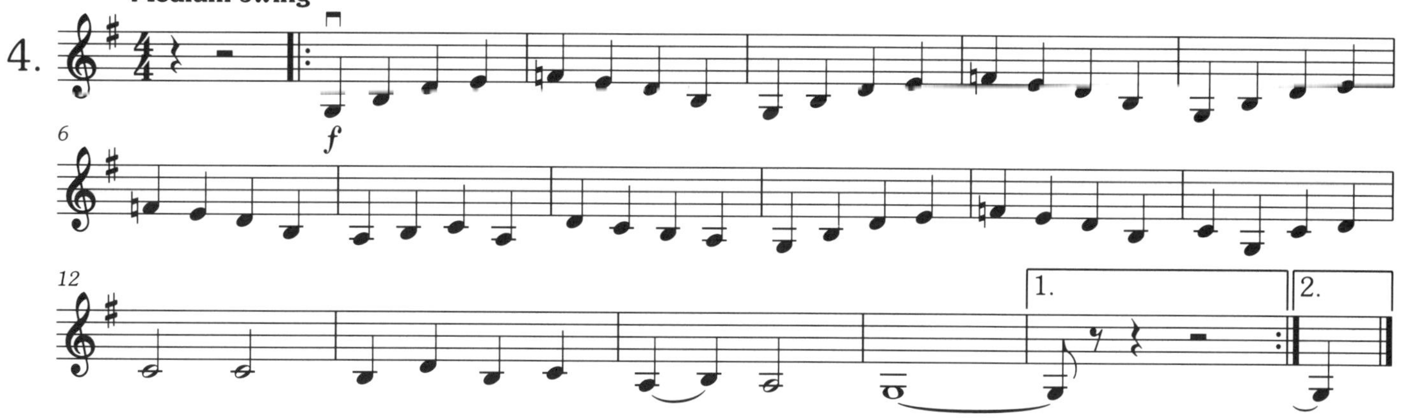

The key of C major

Music in C major has a key signature of no sharps or flats

Observe the rests if playing with viola or cello

Scale and arpeggio of C major

Biddy Biddy

Traditional

Easy tempo

mf

mf

Look for scale patterns

Round the scale

(1) (2)

This means rest for 3 whole bars, so count ① 2, ② 2, ③ 2 and then play from bar 4

The teddy bears' picnic

JOHN W. BRATTON

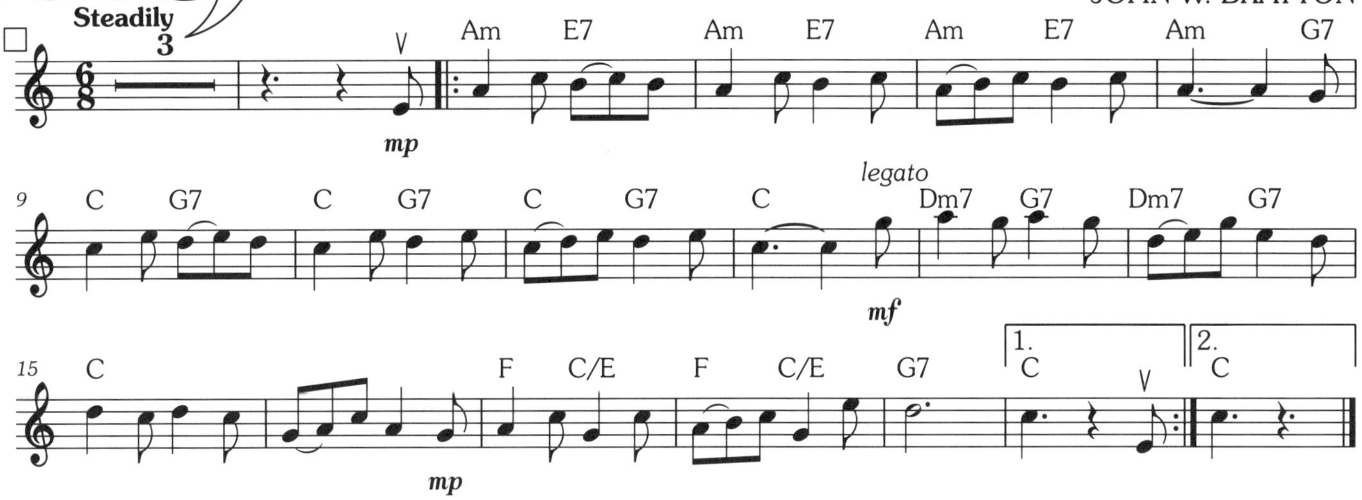

Steadily
3
mp
Am E7 Am E7 Am E7 Am G7
9
C G7 C G7 C G7 C
legato
Dm7 G7 Dm7 G7
mf
15
C F C/E F C/E G7
1. C
2. C
mp

Country gardens

4 clicks intro

Traditional

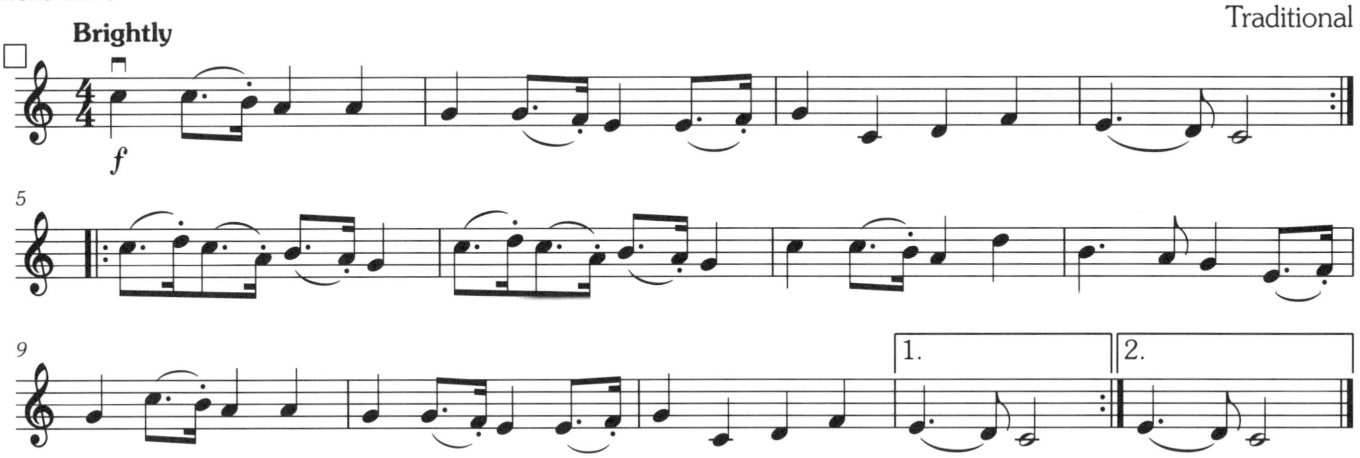

Brightly
f
5
9
1.
2.

Summer is icumen in

Round

Traditional

Sunnily
(1)
(2)
(3)
f
(4)

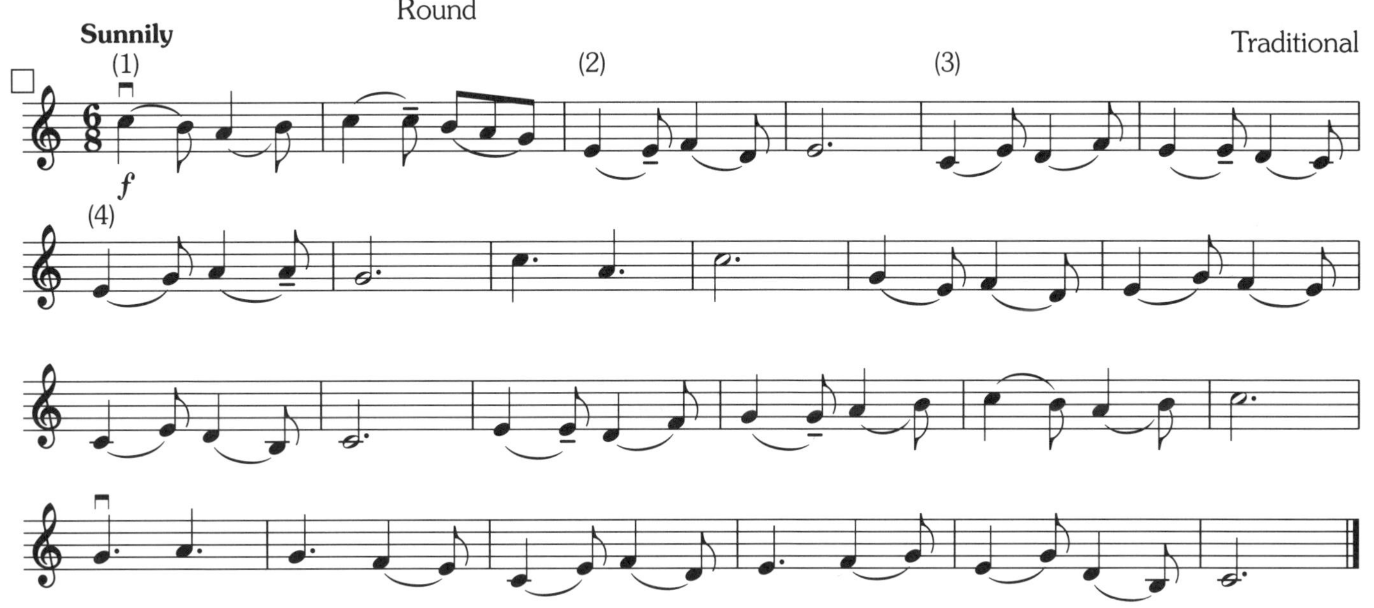

Abschied

6 clicks intro

Traditional

Langsam
3.
p
1.
2.
p
Langsam
4.
pizz.
p
1.
2.
arco
p
pizz.

Intervals

Study in C

Over the rainbow

Touch the notes lightly with the 4th finger to play the harmonics

Harmonics

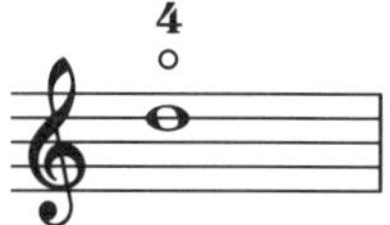

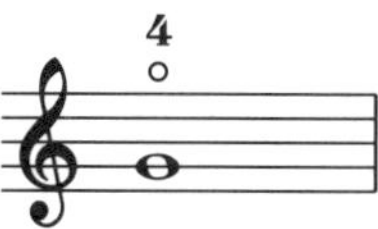

Pearls

Wistfully

pp

pp

Using the 4th finger

This 4th finger makes the same sound as the E string

Step round

At a steady pace

Whither blows the wind

Moderately

Play some of your tunes from Book 1 using 4th finger instead of open strings

CROTCHET TRIPLETS mean that three crotchets are played in the time of one minim

Oh, Lady be good!

Music and Lyrics by GEORGE GERSHWIN and IRA GERSHWIN

4 clicks intro

Slow and graceful

The keys of Canterbury

Oh, how lovely is the evening

Round

Polovtsian dance

Barn dance

Waltz from The Merry Widow

6 clicks intro

FRANZ LEHÁR (1870–1948)

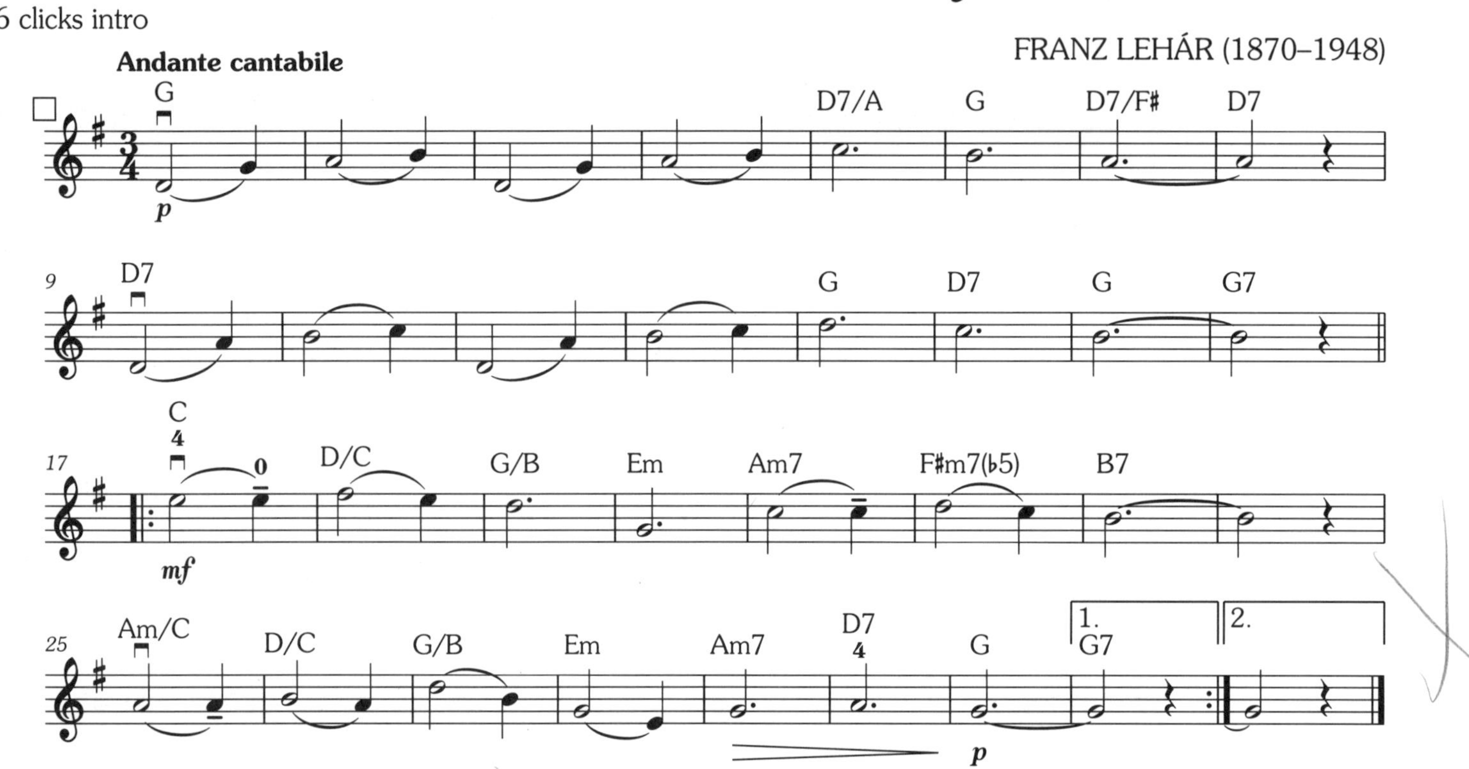

Oh! Susannah

4 clicks intro

STEPHEN C. FOSTER (1826–1864)

Scale and arpeggio of G major
(2 octaves)

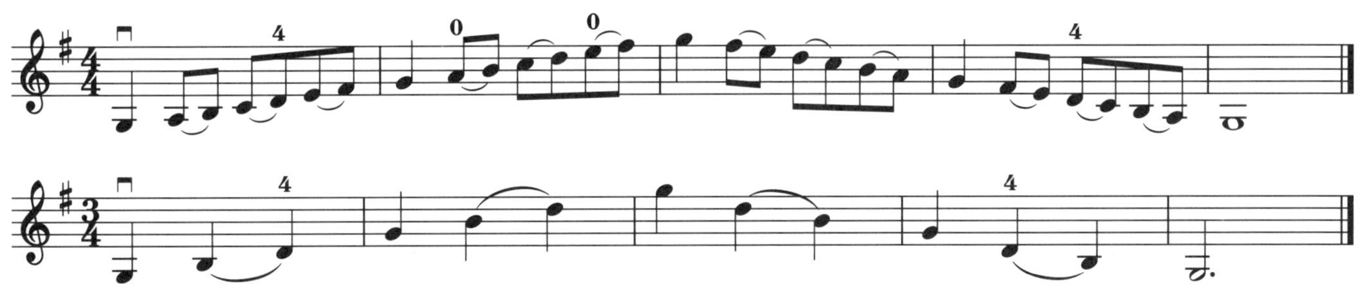

Etude 1

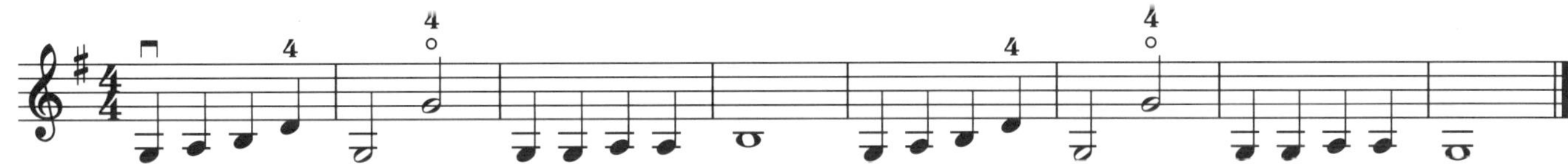

Etude 2

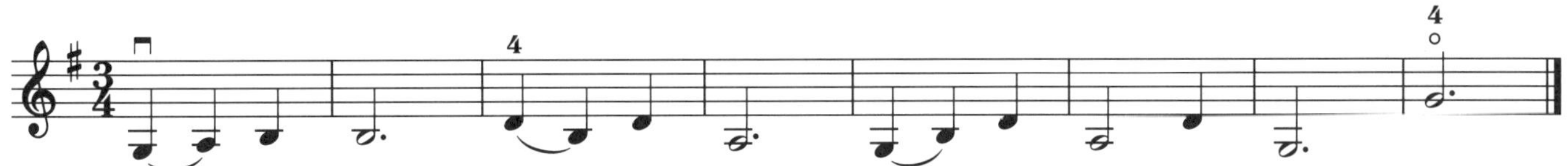

Soliloquy

Camptown races
4 clicks intro
Lively
STEPHEN C. FOSTER (1826–1864)
mf
f
mf
COL LEGNO means tap the strings
with the wood of the bow
Hickory, dickory, dock!
Steadily
Traditional
mf
Col legno
mf

Black Forest

Fits with *German Tune* in book 1, page 23

Summer's end

Fits with *Autumn* in book 1, page 21

Caribbean carnival

Fits with *Jamaican dance* in book 1, page 49

High B

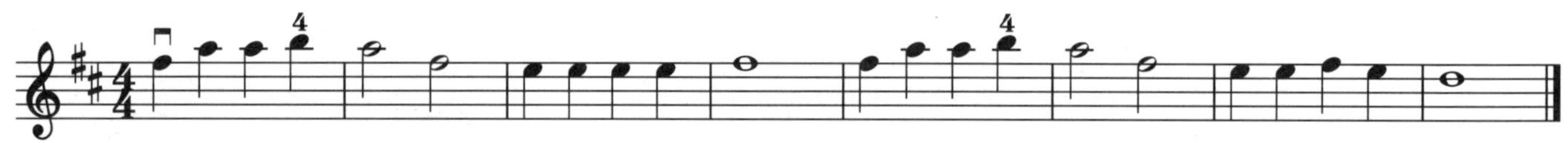

Marie's wedding

4 clicks intro

Cindy

Cheekily

Traditional

The girl I left behind me

4 clicks intro

Traditional

The northern lights of old Aberdeen

MARY WEBB

Gracefully

Hot cross buns

Decisively

Traditional

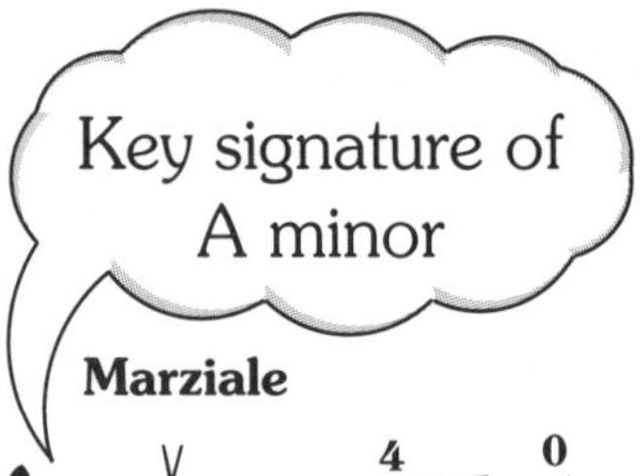

f *p* *f*

Key signature of A minor

When Johnny comes marching home

Marziale

Traditional

mf

God save the Queen

Nobly

Traditional

Believe me, if all those endearing charms

5 ♪ clicks intro

THOMAS MOORE (1779–1852)

Poignantly

1.

Poignantly

2.

Poignantly

3.

Poignantly

4.

The key of F major

The note B♭

Music in F major has a key signature of ONE flat

The FLAT lowers the pitch of a note by one semitone

Barcarolle

JACQUES OFFENBACH (1819–1880)

Triste

Round

Make up your own tunes using the notes G, A, B♭, C and D

Edelweiss

Words by OSCAR HAMMERSTEIN II
Music by RICHARD RODGERS

Upper B♭

Acapulco Bay

4 clicks intro

Fits with *Acapulco Bay* in Flute and Oboe books (pages 6 and 7)

Slur round

Fits with *Step round* in Flute and Oboe books (page 8)

Skip to my Lou

Traditional

Lullaby

6 clicks intro

Fits with *Lullaby* in Brass, Woodwind and Percussion books (page 14)

Slowly

1.

Slowly

2.

Slowly

3.

Slowly

4.

O little town of Bethlehem

Fits with *O little town of Bethlehem* in Brass, Woodwind and Percussion books (page 49)
This melody can also be used with the accompaniment part in Team Strings book 1 (page 45)

3 clicks intro

Moderato Traditional

1.

6

Moderato

2.

6

Moderato

3.

6

Moderato

4.

6

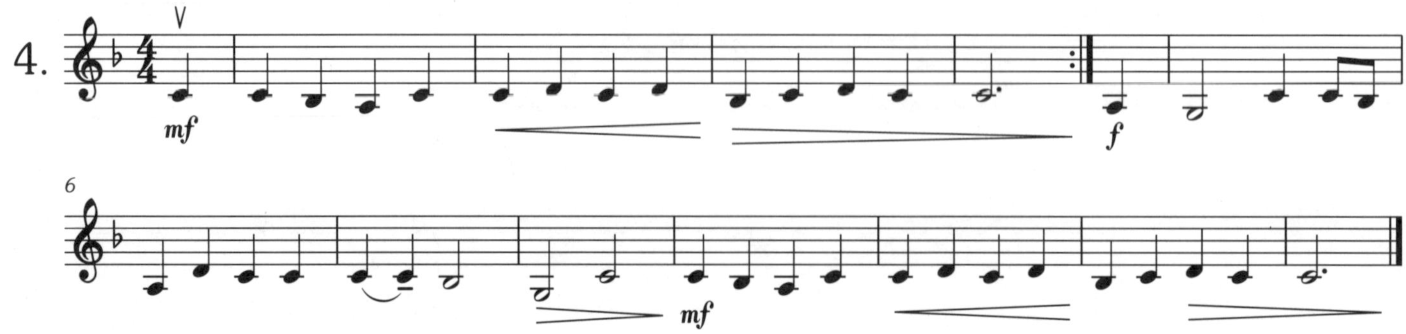

Upper F

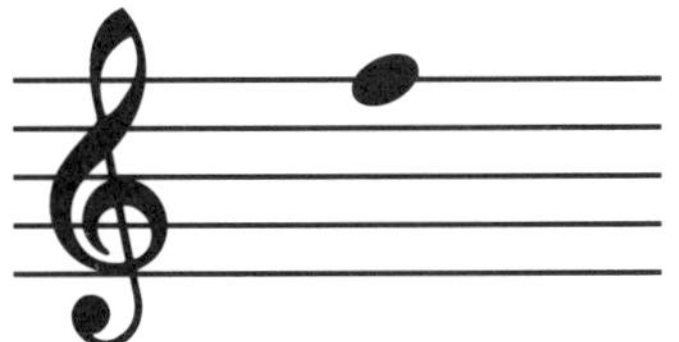

Scale and arpeggio of F major

Little boy blue

Traditional

With a lilt

p

Fight the good fight

JOHN L. HATTON (1808–1886)

Brightly

f

Liza Jane

4 clicks intro

Traditional

Breezily

Pentatonic improvisation

Pentatonic scale on D

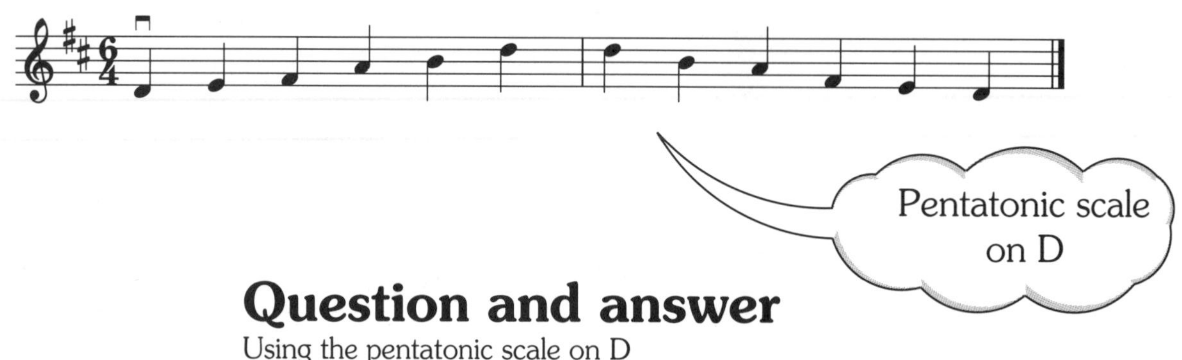

Question and answer

Using the pentatonic scale on D

Continue

Continue

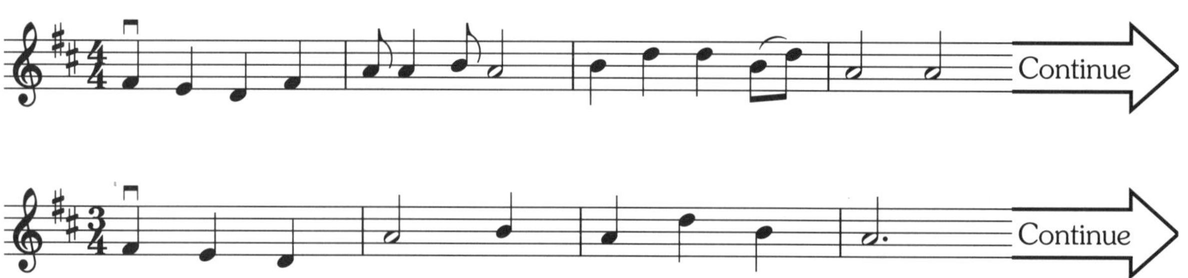

I know the Lord's laid his hands on me

7 clicks intro

Traditional

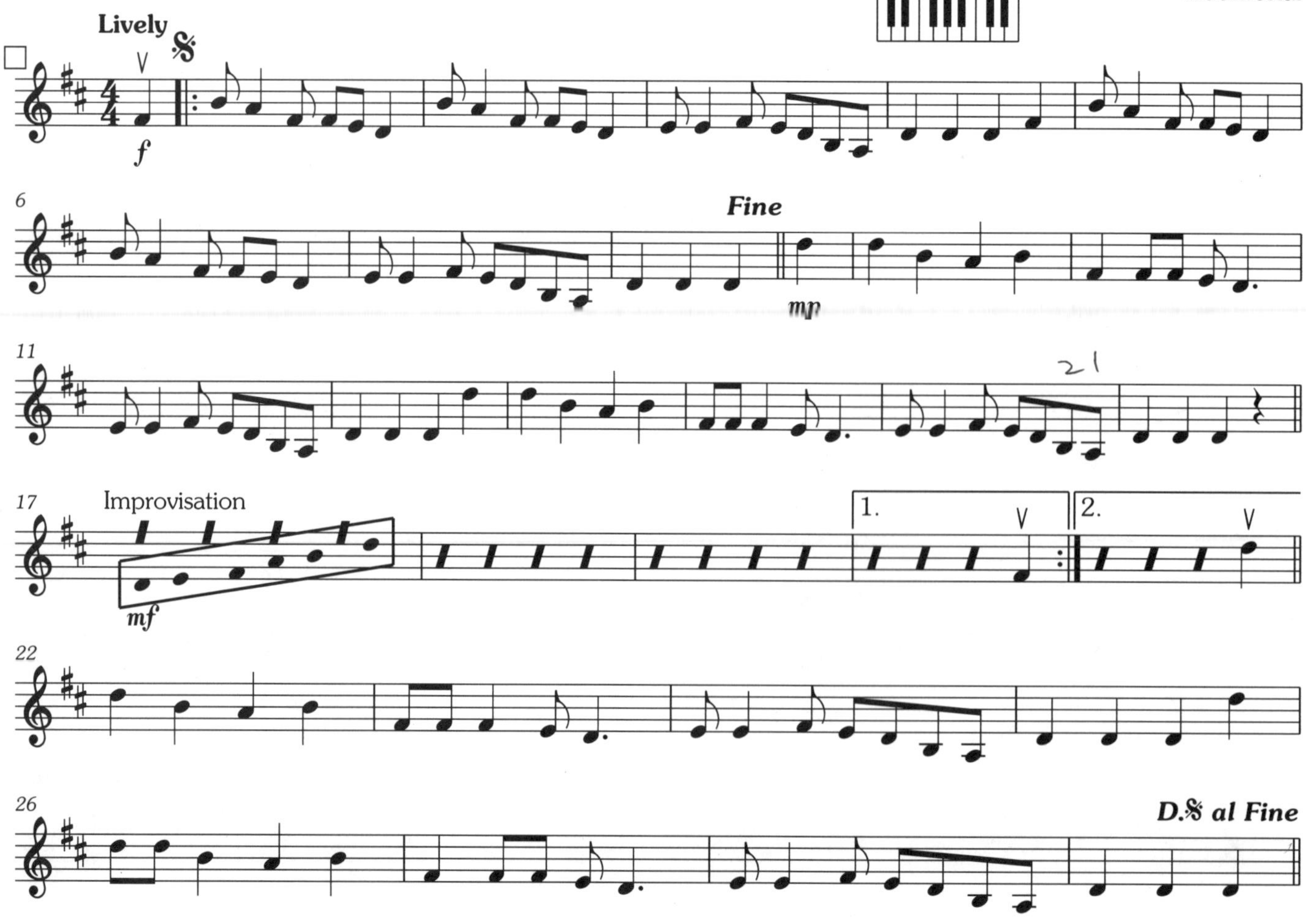

Lively
f
6
Fine
mp
11
17
Improvisation
mf
1.
2.
22
26
D.𝄋 al Fine

Caribbean dance

7 clicks intro

Traditional

Tempo di Rumba

1\.

f

Fine

p

D.C. al Fine

Tempo di Rumba

2\.

f

Fine

p

D.C. al Fine

Tempo di Rumba

3\.

f

Fine

p

D.C. al Fine

The key of B♭ major

The notes E♭ and Upper E♭

Music in B♭ major has a key signature of TWO flats

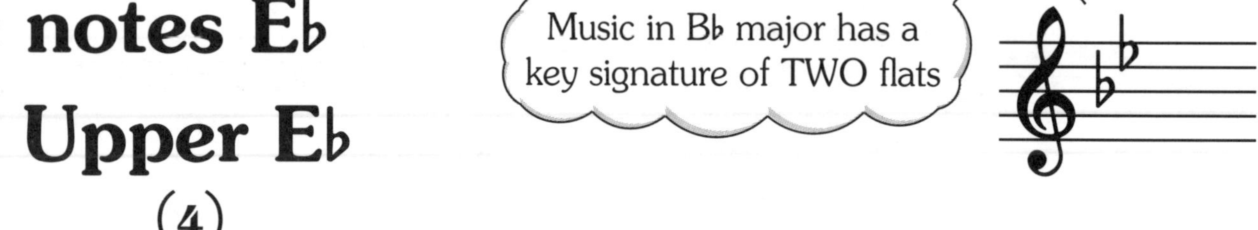

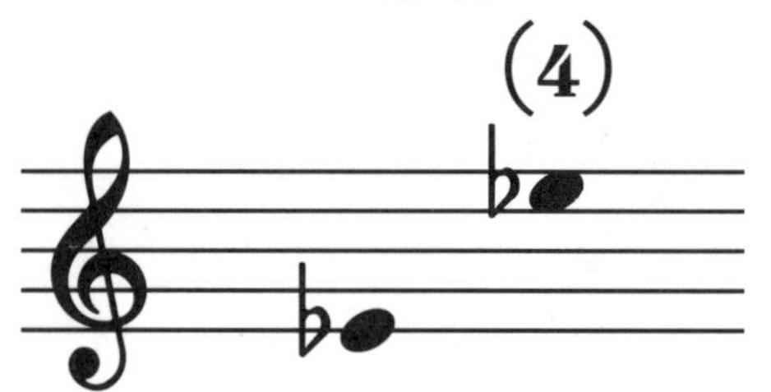

Scale and arpeggio of B♭ major (low)

John Brown's body

Marziale

Traditional

Scale and arpeggio of B♭ major (high)

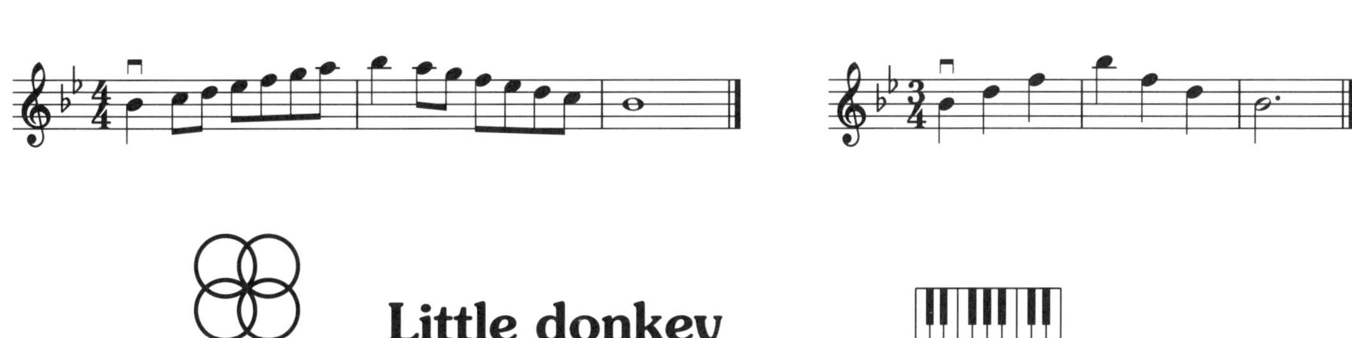

Little donkey

Fits with *Little donkey* in Brass, Woodwind and Percussion books (page 37)

4 clicks intro

Words and Music by ERIC BOSWELL

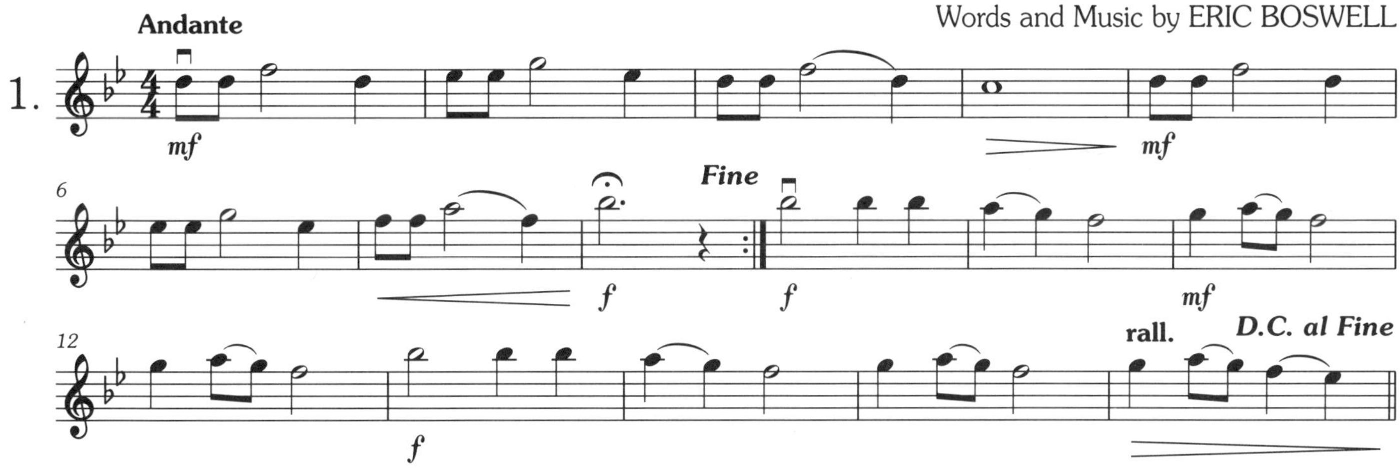

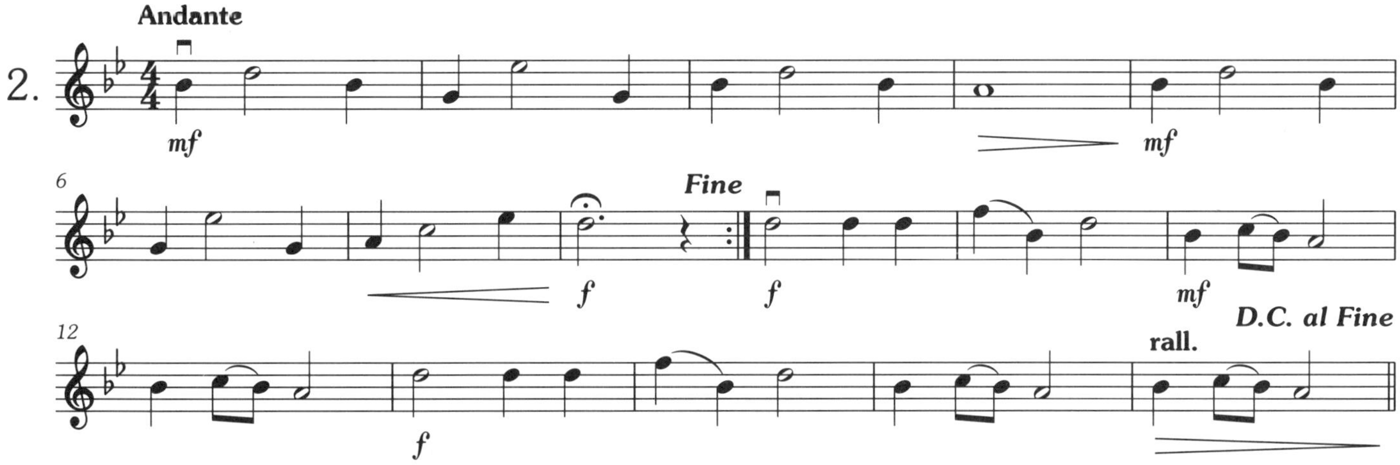

Andante
1.
mf
mf
6
Fine
f
f
mf
12
rall.
D.C. al Fine
f

Andante
2.
mf
mf
6
Fine
f
f
mf
12
D.C. al Fine
rall.
f

Andante
3.
mf
mf
6
Fine
f
f
mf
12
rall.
D.C. al Fine
f

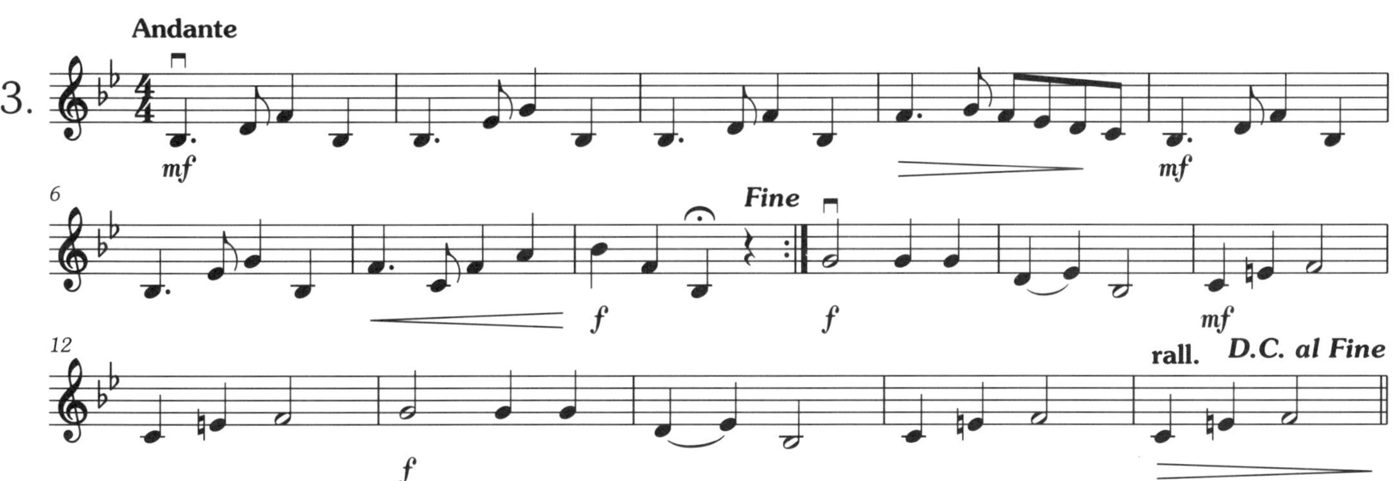

Pomp and circumstance

EDWARD ELGAR (1857–1934)

Blowin' in the wind

Fits with *Blowin' in the wind* in Brass, Woodwind and Percussion books (page 21)

4 clicks intro

Words and Music by BOB DYLAN

Steadily

1. *mf* 1. 7 2. 14 *f* 21

Steadily

2. *mf* 1. 7 2. 14 *f* 21

Steadily

3. *mf* 1. 7 2. 14 *f* 21

Third position

The magic carpet

Fits with *The wizard* in Team Strings book 1 (page 43)

Etude

The notes high C♯ and high D

High C♯

High D

Pease pudding hot

Traditional

Scale and arpeggio of D major (2 octaves)

Song and dance

Fits with *Song and dance* in Team Strings book 1 (page 26)

Traditional

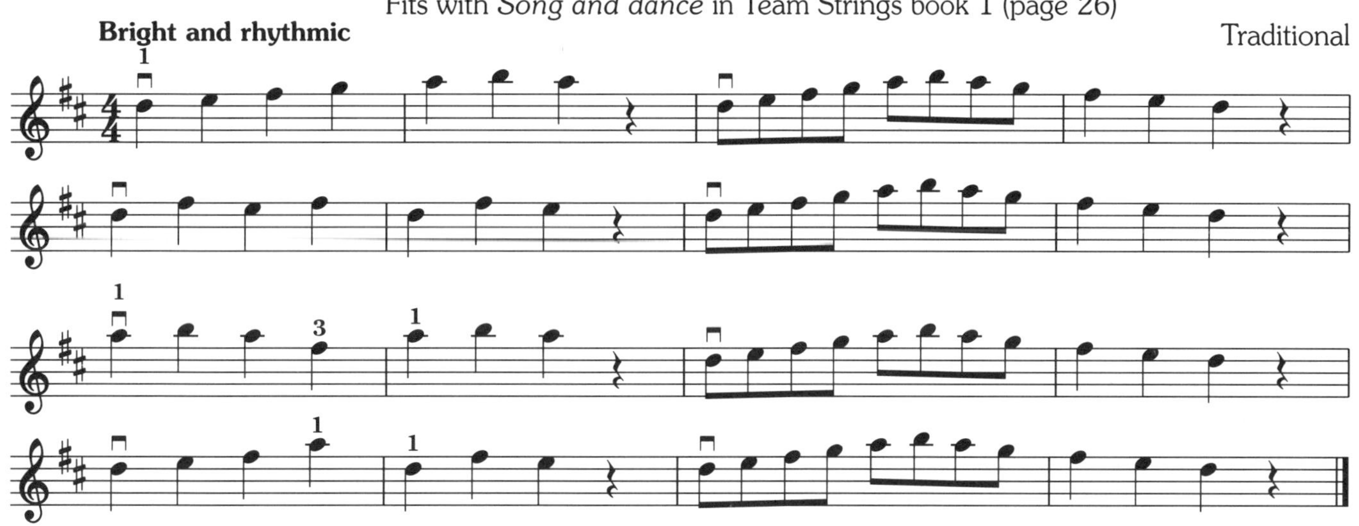

The key of A major

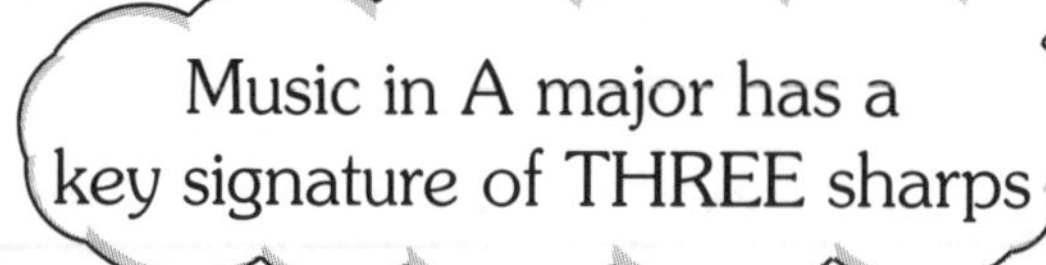

Low C♯

Row, row, row the boat

Round

Traditional

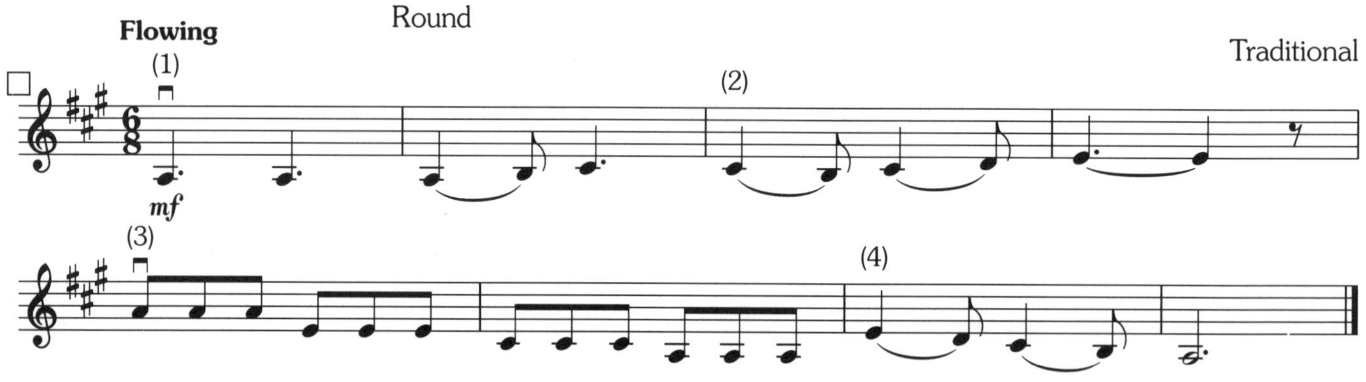

Shortnin' bread

4 clicks intro

Traditional

The note G♯

Scale and arpeggio of A major
(2 octaves)

All made up

Victorian ballad

Slow waltz tempo

f

Fine

mp

D.C. al Fine

Auld lang syne

4 clicks intro

Traditional

Hoe down

4 clicks intro

Molly Wicks and the pupils of Greenmeadow Junior School

Scale and arpeggio of D minor harmonic (2 octaves)

D minor round

The truth from above

3 clicks intro

Traditional

Charlie is my darling

Traditional

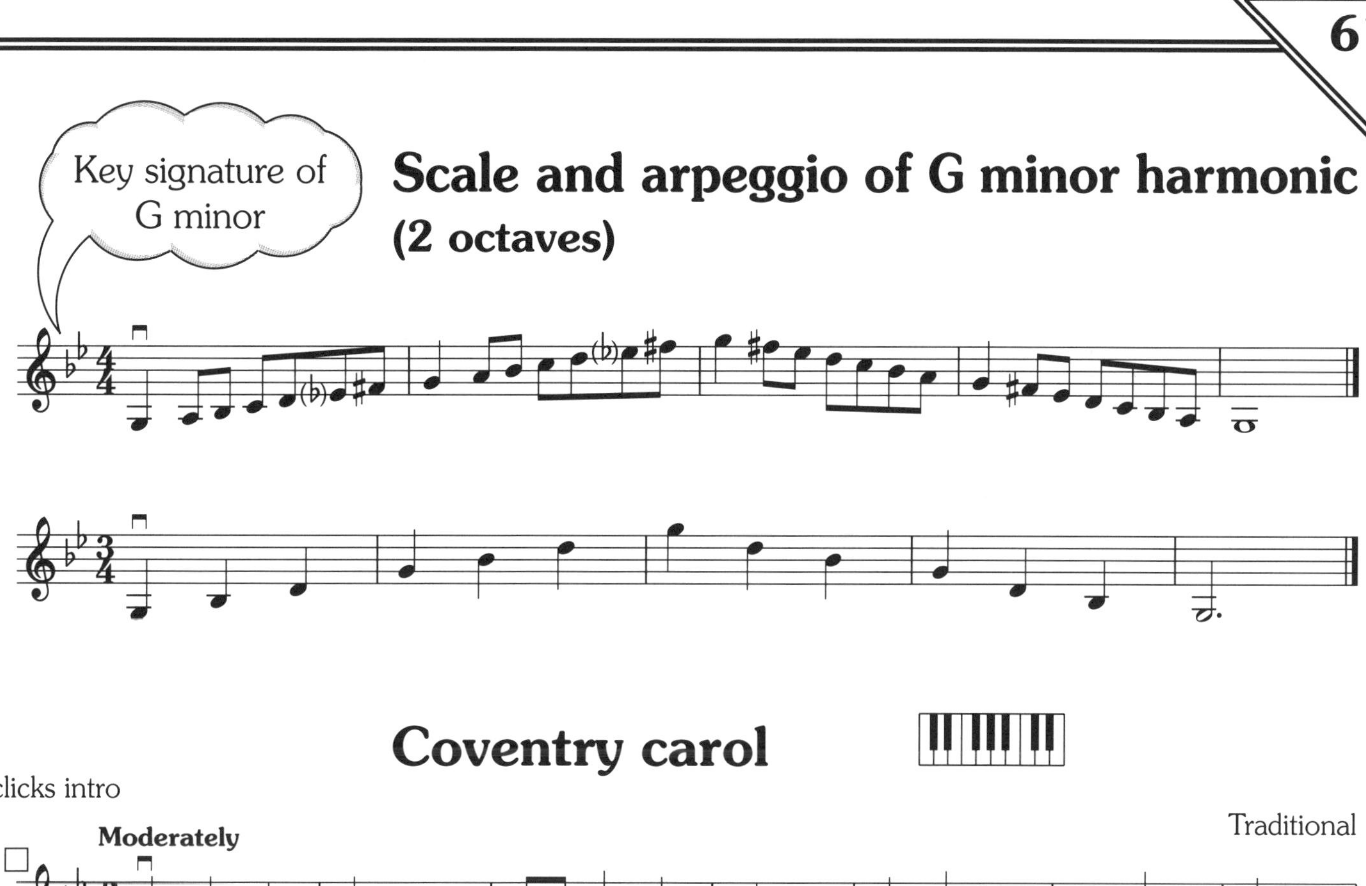

Scale and arpeggio of G minor harmonic (2 octaves)

Coventry carol

3 clicks intro

Traditional

Moderately

mf

Summertime

6 clicks intro

Music and Lyrics by GEORGE GERSHWIN, DUBOSE and DOROTHY HEYWARD and IRA GERSHWIN

Moderately, with expression

Star wars

4 clicks intro

JOHN WILLIAMS

Allegro assai

1. to Coda D.𝄋 al Coda CODA

Allegro assai

2. to Coda D.𝄋 al Coda CODA

Allegro assai
3.
f
to Coda
mf
D.S. al Coda
ff
CODA
ff
Allegro assai
4.
f
to Coda
mf
f
D.S. al Coda
ff
CODA
ff

My heart will go on

Love theme from *Titanic*

4 clicks intro

Words by W. JENNINGS
Music by JAMES HORNER

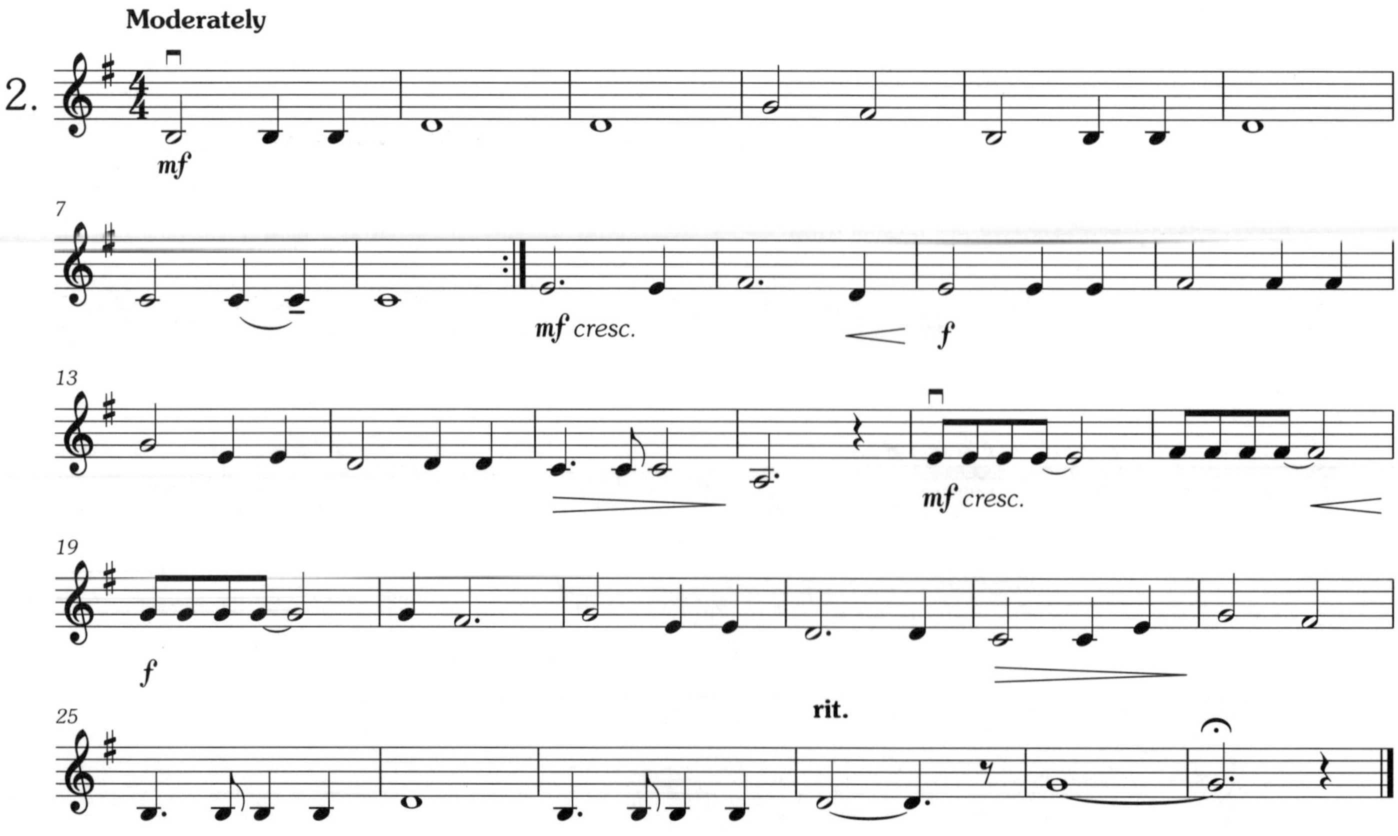

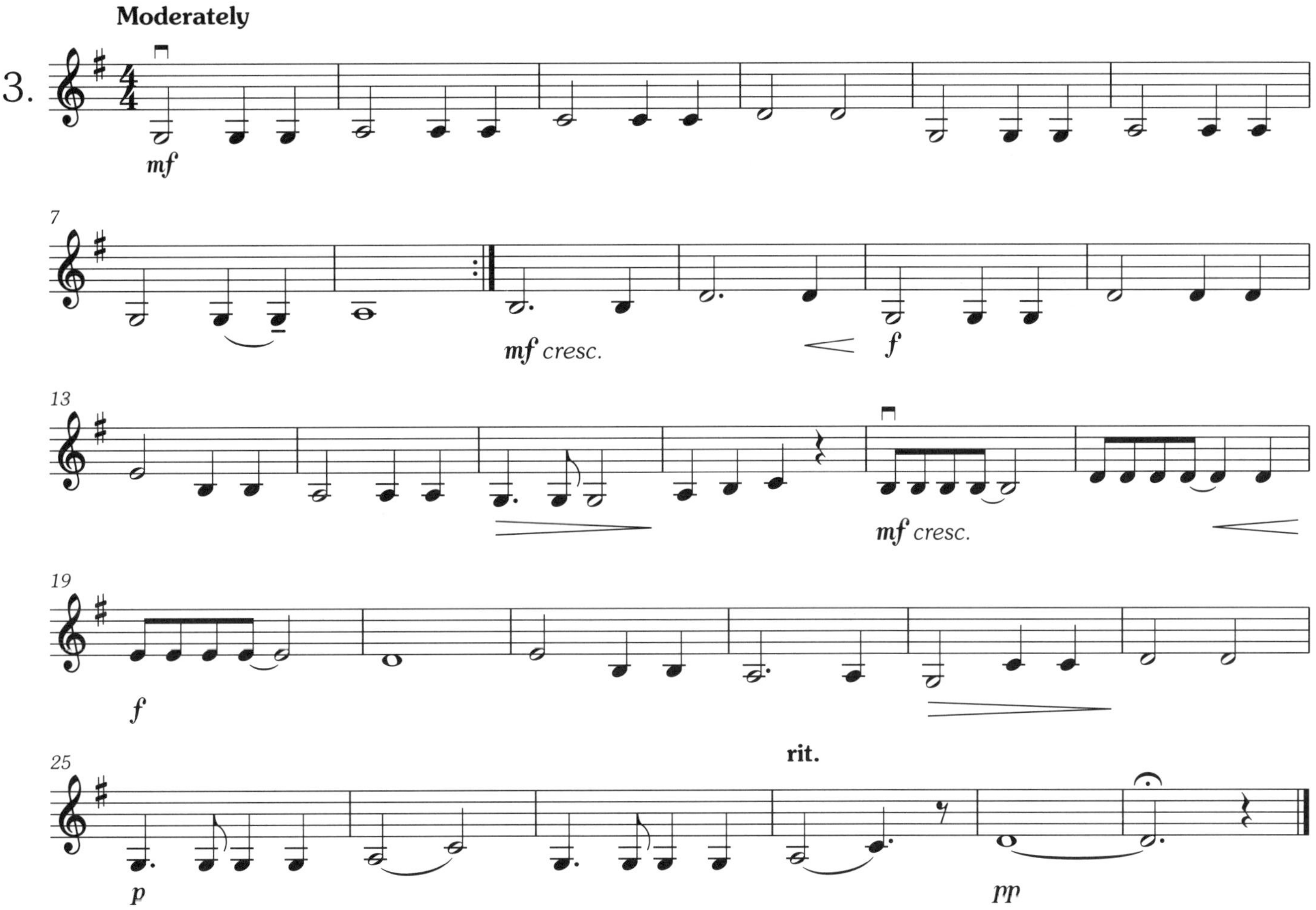

Moderately

3.

mf

mf cresc.

f

mf cresc.

f

rit.

p

pp

Eternal Father, strong to save

3 clicks intro

Words by W. WHITING
Music by J.B. DYKES (1823–1876)

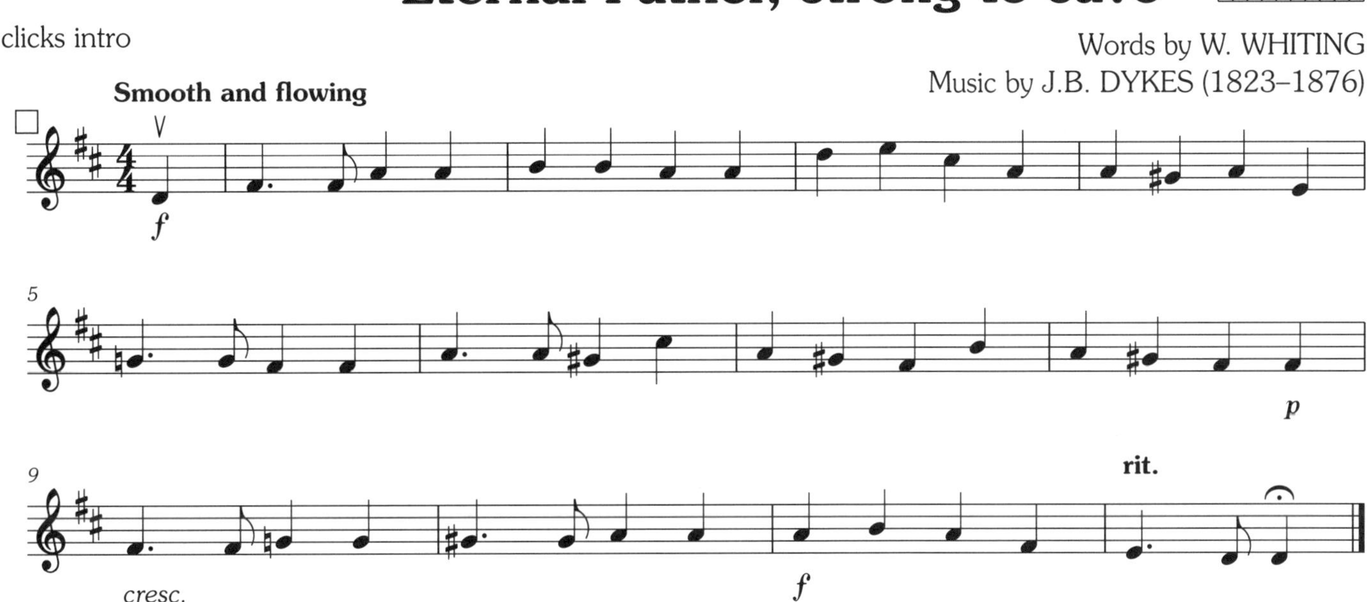

Pink Panther

7 clicks intro

HENRY MANCINI

GRADE 3

The 2005–2007 Syllabus should be read for details of requirements, especially those for scales, aural tests and sight-reading. Attention should be paid to the Special Notices on the inside front cover, where warning is given of any changes.

The syllabus is obtainable from music retailers or from the Services Department, The Associated Board of the Royal Schools of Music, 24 Portland Place, London W1B 1LU, United Kingdom (please send a stamped addressed C5 (162mm × 229mm) envelope).

In exam centres outside the UK, information and syllabuses may be obtained from the Local Representative.

REQUIREMENTS

SCALES AND ARPEGGIOS (from memory)
in E major; E minor (one octave)
G, A, B♭, D majors; G, A, D minors (two octaves)

Scales
in the above keys (minors in melodic *or* harmonic form at candidate's choice):
(i) separate bows
(ii) slurred, two quavers to a bow

Chromatic Scales
starting on open strings G, D and A (one octave):
separate bows, even notes

Arpeggios
the common chords of the above keys:
(i) separate bows, even notes
(ii) slurred, three notes to a bow

Dominant Sevenths
in the keys of C, G and D (starting on open strings G, D and A and resolving on the tonic) (one octave):
separate bows, even notes

PLAYING AT SIGHT (see current syllabus)

AURAL TESTS (see current syllabus)

THREE PIECES *page*

Candidates must prepare three pieces, one from each of the three Lists, A, B and C. Candidates may choose from the pieces printed in this volume or any other piece listed for the grade. A full list is given in the current syllabus.

Music origination by Andrew Jones.

Cover by Økvik Design.

Printed in England by Caligraving Ltd, Thetford, Norfolk.

Where appropriate, pieces in this volume have been checked with original source material and edited as necessary for instructional purposes. Fingering, phrasing, bowing, metronome marks and the editorial realization of ornaments (where given) are for guidance only; they are not comprehensive or obligatory.

Rigaudon and Trio

from *Water Music*, Suite No. 3 in G, HWV 350

Transcribed and edited by
Richard Jones

HANDEL

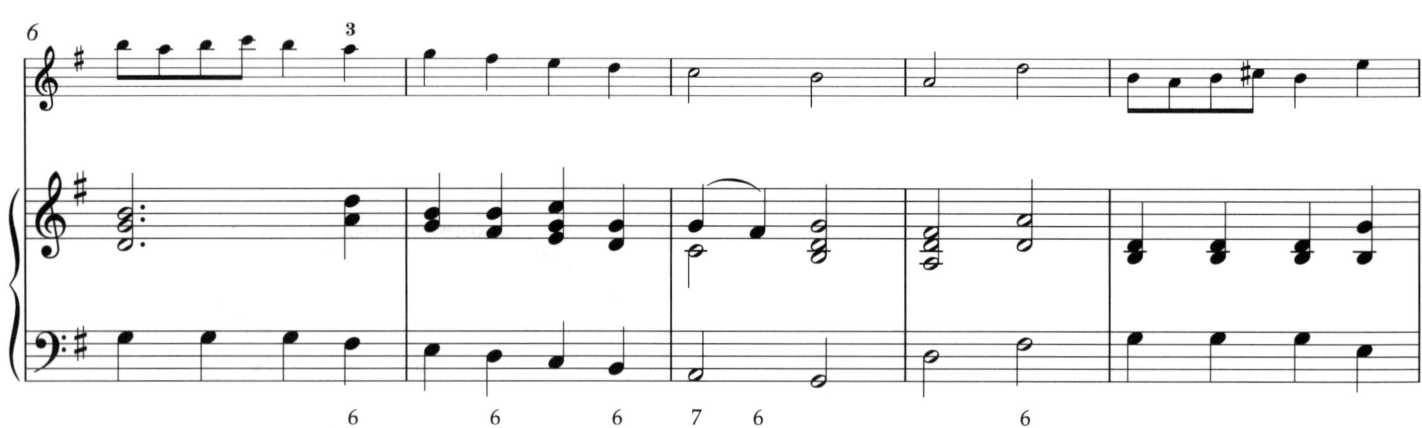

This rigaudon and trio are drawn from the third of the three orchestral suites that make up Handel's *Water Music*. This collection of pieces takes its name from the circumstances of its first performance: a royal water party on the River Thames on 17 July 1717, accompanied by Handel's music, 'which His Majesty liked so well that he caused it to be played over three times in going and returning.' The rigaudon is a lively French dance in duple time, similar to the bourrée. This rigaudon was originally scored for oboes, strings and continuo. The slurs are authentic, but all dynamics are editorial suggestions only. Crotchets might be lightly detached (without lifting the bow off the string). In the exam the da capo should be played, but none of the internal repeats.
Sources: *The Celebrated Water Musick in seven parts* (London: J. Walsh, *c.*1733);
Handel's Celebrated Water Musick compleat: set for the harpsicord (London: J. Walsh, 1743)

16
p
p
21
mf
mf
27
f
f
33
Fine

TRIO

Watkins' Ale

A:2

Arranged by
Edward Huws Jones

ANON. ENGLISH

This delightful and rather cheeky Elizabethan melody and its variations are adapted from versions in the 'Fitzwilliam Virginal Book' and the 'Welde Lute Book'. Your performance can be as lively as you like; the rhythm in bb. 13–16 needs to be crisp. EHJ

A:3

Moderato

First movement from Sonatina, Anh. 5/1

Arranged by
Eta Cohen and Richard Drakeford

BEETHOVEN

The young Beethoven received piano and violin lessons from his father, and made his first public appearance at a concert in 1778, at the age of seven. This Moderato is taken from a pair of sonatinas for piano, listed as Anhang (appendix) 5 in G. Kinsky and H. Halm: *Das Werk Beethovens*.

17
mp
mp
21
25
mf
mf
29
f
f

B:1

Romance

No. 3 from *Eight Easy Pieces*

BAKLANOVA

From Edition Peters No. 5703 Baklanova: *Eight Easy Pieces*

28
cresc.
34
f
p
41
mf
48
56
rit.

B:2

Waltz

Op. 39 No. 15

Arranged by
Shin'ichi Suzuki

BRAHMS

Brahms's Op. 39 Waltzes were originally written for piano duet, then adapted by him for piano solo. They celebrate a dance form associated with Vienna, his adopted city.

21
poco rit. a tempo
f
p
27
p
poco cresc.
33
poco rit. a tempo
f
pp
39
poco rit.

B:3

Air de ballet

No. 4 from *Petite école de la mélodie*, Op. 123, Book 1

C. DANCLA

The violinist Charles Dancla (1817–1907) was a member of a very musical family. His two brothers and sister were accomplished musicians, and the four players formed a chamber group that performed regularly in Paris in the 1840s. Some of the dynamics in this edition have been added for guidance.

20
mp
sim.
25
f
mp
cresc.
mp cresc.
f
31
p
36
41

C:1

Down by the Riverside

Arranged by
Edward Huws Jones

ANON. SPIRITUAL

This well-known spiritual begins: 'Gonna lay down my sword and shield, down by the riverside... Ain't gonna study war no more.' This bluesy arrangement of the tune needs a relaxed bowing style and swung quavers. EHJ

20
f
f
24
29
mp
cresc.
mp
cresc.
33
1.
2.
mf
f
f

C:2

Shepherdess

from *Folk Melodies*

Arranged by
Helena Dunicz-Niwińska and Maria Dziewulska

LUTOSŁAWSKI

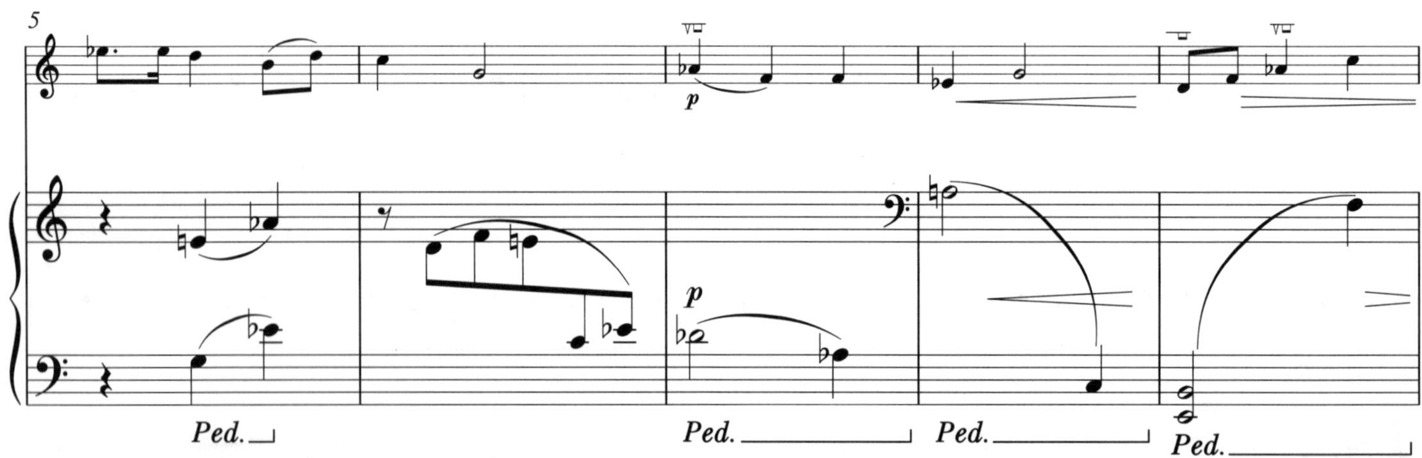

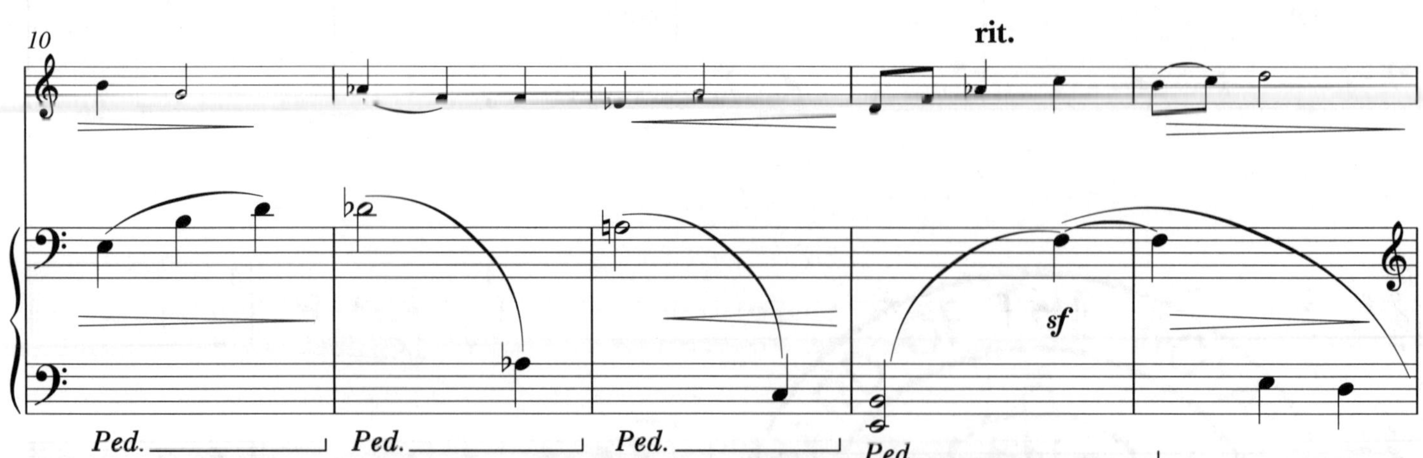

This piece by Polish composer Witold Lutosławski (1913–94) is based on a folk-tune from the Podlasie region in the east of the country, known for its forests and wetlands. The bowing symbols indicate the following:

- with the lower part of the bow
- with the whole bow

Meno mosso
Tempo I
pp
p
mf
Ped.
rit.
sf
Meno mosso
rit.
Lento

C:3

Ain't Misbehavin'

Arranged by
Edward Huws Jones

WALLER and BROOKS

Lazy swing (♫ = ♩ ♪ triplet) [♩ = c.104]

5

9

14

Ain't Misbehavin' is a classic jazz tune from the 1920s. The style calls for a natural, relaxed use of the bow, sometimes slurring across the beat. As is often the case in jazz, the quavers should be swung. EHJ

19
mf
cresc.
mf
cresc.
23
f
dim.
mf
f
dim.
mf
28
p
p
32
1.
2.
f
f
f
f
8